Montgomery Pike

Explorer and Military Officer

Zebulon Montgomery Pike

Explorer and Military Officer

by Steve Walsh

Filter Press, LLC
Palmer Lake, Colorado

Zebulon Montgomery Pike:
Explorer and Military Officer

by Steve Walsh

Published by Filter Press, LLC, in cooperation with
Denver Public Schools and Colorado Humanities

ISBN: 978-0-86541-123-4
LCCN: 2011924863

Produced with the support of Colorado Humanities and the
National Endowment for the Humanities. Any views, findings,
conclusions, or recommendations expressed in this publication
do not necessarily represent those of the National Endowment
for the Humanities or Colorado Humanities.

Cover portrait courtesy of Denver Public Library, Western
History Collection, Z-8951.

Printed in the United States of America

Great Lives in Colorado History Series

Contents

Pike joined the U. S. Army at age 15. Later, he led his men on expeditions through Louisiana, Missouri, Kansas, and Colorado. He rose to the rank of brigadier general.

Zebulon Pike, Explorer

Do you know the song, "America the Beautiful"? The words to the song were written in 1893 after a day trip to the top of Pikes Peak. The first American explorer to try an **ascent** of Pikes Peak did not make it to the top. His name was Zebulon Montgomery Pike. Pike and his men barely survived terrible winter conditions while trying to climb to the top in 1806. They turned back before reaching the top of the mountain. Pikes Peak is named after Zebulon Pike, even though he never saw the beautiful views from the top of the mountain.

Young Zebulon

Zebulon Montgomery Pike was born in Lamberton, New Jersey, in 1779. He was one of four children in his family. His father, Major Zebulon Pike, helped win several battles in the **American Revolutionary War**. The war lasted from 1775 to 1783. Zebulon was born during the Revolutionary War.

When Zebulon Pike was a boy, his father took the family to live in a distant frontier fort located in Ohio, called Fort Washington. It was a rugged place to live. The area had many wild animals, steep rocky hills, thick forests, rushing rivers, and a doctor who treated people only when they were badly hurt. Many Native Americans lived nearby. The family's army experience influenced young Zebulon. He learned many outdoor skills living on the frontier, such as hunting, fishing, and **tracking.** He used these skills later when he led **expeditions** to explore new areas.

Military Career

Zebulon wanted to become a soldier like his father. He joined the United States Army at the age of fifteen. Soon after, his army unit went on a dangerous mission to regain land from Native Americans in the Battle of Fallen Timbers in 1794. One thousand United States soldiers fought against 500 Native Americans. The soldiers won, and they built several new forts along the Ohio River. Major Zebulon Pike was in charge of one of the new forts. Zebulon was ordered to other military forts and worked in the supply departments for the next four years. He met his wife, Clarissa, at an army fort. They were married in 1801. They had several children, but only one daughter survived. His family lived with him at the forts, but they were unable to go with him on his dangerous expeditions.

A very important event occurred at this time in American history. The emperor of France, Napoleon Bonaparte, offered to sell all the land between the Mississippi River and the Rocky Mountains to the United States. The Americans accepted the offer and, suddenly, the size of the United States was doubled. The **territory** was called the Louisiana Purchase. In 1804, President Thomas Jefferson sent two explorers named Lewis and Clark to explore the northern part of the new territory. In 1805, General James Wilkinson sent Zebulon Pike to find the **source** of the Mississippi River.

Pike and his men were supposed to return to St. Louis before winter started, but they stayed longer throughout the cold weather. His soldiers had little food and only a few pieces of equipment. They paddled a 75-foot wooden boat against a strong current up the Mississippi River. At times, they had to pull the heavy boat up the river with ropes.

AN ACCOUNT OF EXPEDITIONS

TO THE

Sources of the Mississippi,

AND THROUGH THE

WESTERN PARTS OF LOUISIANA,

TO THE SOURCES OF THE

ARKANSAW, KANS, LA PLATTE, AND PIERRE JAUN, RIVERS:

PERFORMED BY ORDER OF THE

GOVERNMENT OF THE UNITED STATES

DURING THE YEARS 1805, 1806, AND 1807.

AND A TOUR THROUGH

THE

INTERIOR PARTS OF NEW SPAIN,

WHEN CONDUCTED THROUGH THESE PROVINCES,

BY ORDER OF

THE CAPTAIN-GENERAL,

IN THE YEAR 1807.

By MAJOR Z. M. PIKE.

ILLUSTRATED BY MAPS AND CHARTS.

PHILADELPHIA:

PUBLISHED BY C. & A. CONRAD, & Co. No. 30, CHESNUT STREET. SOMER-
VELL & CONRAD, PETERSBURGH. BONSAL, CONRAD, & Co. NORFOLK.
AND FIELDING LUCAS, Jr. BALTIMORE.

John Binns, Printer....1810.

Pike kept a journal in which he wrote about his western expeditions. The journal was published as a book. This journal is titled An Account of Expeditions to the Sources of the Mississippi and through the Western Parts of Louisiana…and a Tour through the Interior Parts of New Spain.

6 *Zebulon Pike*

3d December, Wednesday.—The weather moderating to 3 below 0, our absentees joined, one with his feet frozen, but were not able to bring up the horse; sent two men back on horseback. The hardships of last voyage had now began, and had the climate only been as severe as the climate then was, some of the men must have perished, for they had no winter clothing; I wore myself cotton overalls, for I had not calculated on being out in that inclement season of the year. Dr. Robinson and myself, with assistants, went out and took the altitude of the north mountain, on the base of a mile;* after which, together with Sparks, we endeavoured to kill a *cow* but without effect. Killed two bulls, that the men might use pieces of their hides for mockinsons. Left Sparks out. On our return to camp found the men had got back with the strayed horse, but too late to march.

4th December, Thursday.—Marched about five; took up Sparks who had succeeded in killing a cow. Killed two buffalo and six turkies. Distance 20 miles.

5th December, Friday.—Marched at our usual hour. Passed one very bad place of *falling rocks*; had to carry our loads. Encamped on the main branch of the river, near the entrance of the south mountain. In the evening walked up to the mountain. Heard 14 guns at camp during my absence, which alarmed me considerably; returned as quickly as possible, and found that the cause of my

* The perpendicular height of the mountain from the level of the prairie, was 10,581 feet, and admitting that the prairie was 8000 feet from the level of the sea, it would make the elevation of this peak 18,581 feet, equal to some, and surpassing the calculated height of others, for the peak of Teneriffe and falling short of that of Chimborazo only 1,701 feet. Indeed it was so remarkable as to be known to all the savage nation for hundreds of miles around, and to be spoken of with admiration by the Spaniards of N. Mexico, and was the bounds of their travels N. W. Indeed in our wandering in the mountains, it was never out of our sight, (except when in a valley) from the 14th November to the 27th January.

Zebulon Pike 7

Zebulon did not know what to expect on the long and difficult journey. He and his soldiers wore light cotton coats and pants, lightweight boots, and long shirts. They were very cold because temperatures often fell below zero. Most of the meat they ate came from deer they hunted. Native Americans and British traders helped Zebulon and his men to survive by giving them food and shelter. They did not find the true source of the Mississippi River. However, Zebulon bought land from the Sioux Indians. Later, the cities of Minneapolis and St. Paul, Minnesota, were built on this land.

Soon after Zebulon returned from his exploration of the Mississippi River, General Wilkinson ordered him to explore an area that is now Colorado and New Mexico. He traveled from 1805 to 1806 through the present-day states of Missouri, Kansas, Colorado, and New Mexico. This land was part of the **Louisiana Territory**. Spain owned the land west of this territory. Spanish troops had been told about Pike's expedition and tried to catch him, but failed.

Pikes Peak

After traveling through Missouri and Kansas, Zebulon had been ordered to return to St. Louis before winter arrived, but he kept going west. He and his men came to an area 90 miles south of where the city of Denver is now, near the site of the future town of Pueblo. They built a small log fort there. It was the first American building in Colorado.

Courtesy of DPL, Western History Collection, CHS.J2

In 1806, Zebulon Pike and his men were the first Americans to see the mountain he called Grand Peak. Today, we call this mountain Pikes Peak.

Pike and his men faced very cold and harsh conditions when they tried to climb Pikes Peak in 1806. The trip was so bad that Pike wrote in his journal that no man would ever climb to the summit. This photograph was made of climbers on their way to the summit around 1950.

From the fort, they saw a tall, snow-capped mountain. Zebulon called it Grand Peak. He thought that he could climb to the **summit** in one day. Pike and his men hiked for three days, but they were still ten miles from the summit. Pike wrote that it was impossible for anyone to ever climb to the top because of the deep snow and freezing temperatures. This mountain is now known as Pikes Peak, and many people climb to the top each year.

Exploring Colorado and New Mexico

The soldiers were badly prepared for a cold trip! They had only summer clothes.

Zebulon wrote in his **journal** on December 3, 1806:

> The weather **moderating** to 3 below zero, for they [his soldiers] had no winter clothing. I wore myself cotton overalls for I had not calculated on being out in that **inclement** season of the year.

Their shoes were thin leather moccasins, so many of the soldiers had **frostbitten** feet. In January 1806, the men climbed through the Sangre de Cristo Mountains into the San Luis valley. The temperatures were below zero, and sometimes they walked through snow up to their waists. The soldiers built large campfires at night to stay warm. They traveled only five to ten miles per day, far less than their usual 20 miles a day. Often they had little or no food. Once, they did not eat for three days. The men were starving, extremely cold, and worn out.

They built another fort, south of present-day Alamosa. After a few days, Spanish troops arrived and asked them why they were in Spanish territory. Pike pretended he did not know the land belonged to the Spaniards and went with them to Santa Fe and then to Chihuahua, Mexico, to answer more questions.

The Spanish treated Pike and his men well and let them return to the United States. On the return journey, Zebulon wrote about what he saw at the Spanish forts and towns. This information included how large the forts were, how many soldiers were there, and what types of military walls were built around the forts. His men traded jewelry, food, and **trinkets** with Native Americans during the trip.

Zebulon stayed with his family at the fort in St. Louis for several years. He worked hard in the army and earned the rank of brigadier general. When the War of 1812 started between the United States and Great Britain, Zebulon once again led men into danger. In 1813, during the Battle of York near Toronto, Canada, Brigadier General Pike was killed. He was 34 years old at the time of his death.

Pike's Legacy

Zebulon Pike played an important role in Colorado and American history. He led two important expeditions: to find the source of the Mississippi River and to map new western territories in Colorado and New Mexico. He described huge areas of the American West and helped open the land to future **settlement**. He had very little contact with the American Indians because the territory he explored was **inhabited** by tribes that moved from place to place and did not live in settled villages. He fought bravely during the War of 1812 and died in defense of the United States.

Zebulon was the first American to describe Pikes Peak, which was named after him by later explorers. Many years later, Katharine Lee Bates wrote a poem after she had seen the **inspirational** view from the top of Pikes Peak. Her words were later put to music. We call the song, "America the Beautiful." The first four lines are:

> *Oh! Beautiful for spacious skies,*
> *For amber waves of grain,*
> *For purple mountain majesties*
> *Above the fruited plain!*

Questions to Think About

- Would you, like Pike, be willing to join the army at the age of 15? Why or why not?

- Why did Zebulon Pike think that no one would ever climb to the top of Pike's Peak?

- What would it be like to walk from New Jersey to Colorado and back, the way Pike did?

Questions for Young Chautauquans

- Why am I (or should I be) remembered in history?

- What hardships did I face and how did I overcome them?

- What is my historical context (what else was going on in my time)?

Glossary

American Revolutionary War: a war fought from 1775 to 1783 between the thirteen colonies and Great Britain, also called the American War of Independence.

Ascent: a climb to the top of a mountain.

Expeditions: trips made by a group of people for the purpose of discovery.

Frostbitten: to be injured by frost or extreme cold.

Inclement: stormy and cold.

Inhabited: lived in.

Inspirational: causing strong positive emotions or feelings.

Journal: a daily record of events.

Louisiana Territory: a part of the central United States made up of land purchased from France in 1803.

Moderating: an old-fashioned way to say "warming up."

Settlement: a newly settled place for people to live.

Source: the place where a body or water, such as a stream or river, begins.

Summit: the highest point of a mountain.

Territory: a large area of land.

Tracking: following signs, such as footprints, to find animals and people.

Trinkets: small items of little value.

Timeline

1779
Pike was born in
Lamberton, New Jersey.

1775–1783
American Revolutionary
War was fought.

1793
Pike moved to Fort
Washington, Ohio, with
his father.

1794
Pike joined the United
States Army at the age of 15.
American soldiers defeated
Native Americans in the Battle
of Fallen Timbers.

1801
Pike married
Clarissa Brown.

1805
Pike led Mississippi Valley
Expedition to find the source of
the Mississippi River.

Timeline

1806

Pike led Southwest Expedition to explore and map the Colorado Rocky Mountain region. Explorers Lewis and Clark returned to the East from their expedition into the Northwest.

1812

War of 1812 against Great Britain began. Pike was promoted to rank of brigadier general.

1813

Pike died at the Battle of York.

Bibliography

Calvert, Patricia. *Zebulon Pike—Lost in the Rockies.* New York: Benchmark Books, 2003.

Doak, Robin S. *Zebulon Pike: Explorer and Soldier.* Minneapolis: Compass Point Books, 2006.

Pike National Historic Trail Association. *Pike, The Real Pathfinder.* http://zebulonpike.org.

Pike, Zebulon. *The Expeditions of Zebulon Montgomery Pike Through Louisiana Territory and in New Spain During the Years 1805-6-7.* Minneapolis: Ross & Haines, 1965.

Pike, Zebulon. *The Southwestern Journals of Zebulon Pike.* Albuquerque: University of New Mexico Press, 2006.

Sanford, William, and Carl Green. *Zebulon Pike: Explorer of the Southwest.* Springfield, New Jersey: Enslow Publishers, 1996.

Sinnot, Susan. *The World's Great Explorers.* Chicago: Children's Press, 1990.

Stallones, Jared. *Zebulon Pike and the Explorers of the American Southwest.* New York/Philadelphia: Chelsea House Publishers, 1992.

Witteman, Barbara. *Zebulon Pike: Soldier and Explorer.* Mankato, Minnesota: Bridgestone Books, 2003.

Index

About This Series

In 2008, Colorado Humanities and Denver Public Schools' Social Studies Department began a partnership to bring Colorado Humanities' Young Chautauqua program to DPS and to create a series of biographies of Colorado historical figures written by teachers for young readers. The project was called "Writing Biographies for Young People." Filter Press joined the effort to publish the biographies in 2010.

Teachers attended workshops, learned from Colorado Humanities Chautauqua speakers and authors, and toured three major libraries in Denver: The Hart Library at History Colorado, the Western History/Genealogy Department in the Denver Public Library, and the Blair-Caldwell African American Research Library. Their goal was to write biographies using the same skills we ask of students: identify and locate high-quality sources for research, document those sources, and choose appropriate information from the resources.

What you hold in your hands now is the culmination of these teachers' efforts. With this set of age-appropriate biographies, students will be able to read and research on their own, learning valuable skills of research and writing at a young age. As they read each biography, students gain knowledge and appreciation of the struggles and hardships overcome by people from our past, the time period in which they lived, and why they should be remembered in history.

Knowledge is power. We hope this set of biographies will help Colorado students know the excitement of learning history through biography.

Information about the series can be obtained from any of the three partners:

Filter Press at www.FilterPressBooks.com

Colorado Humanities at www.ColoradoHumanities.org

Denver Public Schools at http://curriculum.dpsk12.org

Acknowledgments

Colorado Humanities and Denver Public Schools acknowledge the many contributors to the Great Lives in Colorado History series. Among them are the following:

The teachers who accepted the challenge of writing the biographies

Margaret Coval, Executive Director, Colorado Humanities

Josephine Jones, Director of Programs, Colorado Humanities

Betty Jo Brenner, Program Coordinator, Colorado Humanities

Michelle Delgado, K–5 Social Studies Coordinator, Denver Public Schools

Elma Ruiz, K–5 Social Studies Coordinator, Denver Public Schools, 2005–2009

Joel' Bradley, Project Coordinator, Denver Public Schools

Translation and Interpretation Services Team, Multicultural Outreach Office, Denver Public Schools

Nelson Molina, ELA Professional Development Trainer/Coach and School Liaison, Denver Public Schools

John Stansfield, storyteller, writer, and Teacher Institute lead scholar

Tom Meier, author and Arapaho historian

Celinda Reynolds Kaelin, author and Ute culture
    expert
National Park Service, Bent's Old Fort National
    Historic Site
Daniel Blegen, author and Bent's Fort expert
Blair-Caldwell African American Research Library
Coi Drummond-Gehrig, Denver Public Library,
    Western History/Genealogy Department
Jennifer Vega, Stephen H. Hart Library, History
    Colorado
Dr. Bruce Paton, author and Zebulon Pike expert
Dr. Tom Noel, author and Colorado historian
Susan Marie Frontczak, Chautauqua speaker and
    Young Chautauqua coach
Mary Jane Bradbury, Chautauqua speaker and Young
    Chautauqua coach
Dr. James Walsh, Chautauqua speaker and Young
    Chautauqua coach
Richard Marold, Chautauqua speaker and Young
    Chautauqua coach
Doris McCraw, author and Helen Hunt Jackson
    subject expert
Kathy Naples, Chautauqua speaker and Doc Susie
    subject expert
Tim Brenner, editor
Debra Faulkner, historian and archivist, Brown Palace
    Hotel
Kathleen Esmiol, author and Teacher Institute speaker
Vivian Sheldon Epstein, author and Teacher Institute
    speaker
Beth Kooima, graphic designer, Kooima Kreations

Zebulon Montgomery Pike

Explorador y oficial militar

Zebulon Montgomery Pike

Explorador y oficial militar

por Steve Walsh

Filter Press, LLC
Palmer Lake, Colorado

Zebulon Montgomery Pike
Explorador y oficial militar
por Steve Walsh

Publicado por Filter Press, LLC, conjuntamente con las
Escuelas Públicas de Denver y Colorado Humanities

ISBN: 978-0-86541-123-4
LCCN: 2011924863

Producido con el apoyo de Colorado Humanities y la Fundación
Nacional para las Humanidades. Las opiniones, resultados,
conclusiones o recomendaciones expresadas en esta publicación,
no representan necesariamente las de la Fundación Nacional para
las Humanidades ni las de Colorado Humanities.

La fotografía de la portada es cortesía de Denver Public Library,
Western History Genealogy, Z-8951

Impreso en los Estados Unidos de América

Grandes vidas de la historia de Colorado

Contenidos

Zebulon Pike se enlistó en el United States Army
(Ejército de los Estados Unidos) a la edad de 15 años.
Más adelante, él dirigió a sus hombres en expediciones
a lo largo de Louisiana, Missouri, Kansas y Colorado.
Ascendió al rango de brigadier general.

Zebulon Pike, explorador

¿Conoces la canción, "America the Beautiful" ("America la hermosa")? La letra de la canción fue escrita en 1893 después de un viaje de un día a la **cima** de Pikes Peak (Pico de Pike). El primer explorador norteamericano que intentó **escalar** Pikes Peak no logró llegar a la cumbre. Su nombre era Zebulon Montgomery Pike. Pike y sus hombres apenas lograron sobrevivir las terribles condiciones invernales mientras intentaban escalar hasta la cima en 1806. Se dieron la vuelta antes de alcanzar la cumbre de la montaña. Pikes Peak lleva este nombre en honor a Zebulon Pike, aunque él nunca vio la belleza del paisaje desde la cima de la montaña.

El joven Zebulon

Zebulon Montgomery Pike nació en Lamberton, New Jersey, en 1779. Fue uno de cuatro hijos en su familia. Su padre, el Sargento Mayor Zebulon Pike, ayudó a ganar varias batallas en la **American Revolutionary War (Guerra de la Revolución Norteamericana)**. La guerra duró desde 1775 hasta 1783. Zebulon nació durante la Revolutionary War.

Cuando Zebulon Pike era niño, su padre se llevó a la familia a vivir a un distante fuerte fronterizo situado en Ohio, llamado Fort Washington (Fuerte de Washington). Era un sitio escabroso para vivir. En la zona habían muchos animales salvajes, pronunciadas colinas rocosas, espesos bosques, ríos precipitados y un médico que sólo atendía a las personas cuando estaban gravemente heridas. Muchos indígenas norteamericanos

vivían en las cercanías. La experiencia militar que vivió la familiar influenció al joven Zebulon. Aprendió muchas habilidades de supervivencia al aire libre en la frontera, tales como la caza, la pesca y el **rastreo**. Utilizó estas habilidades en el futuro cuando lideró **expediciones** para explorar zonas nuevas.

Una carrera militar

Zebulon quería convertirse en soldado como
su padre. Se enlistó en el United States
Army (Ejército de los Estados Unidos) a la
edad de 15 años. Poco después, su unidad se
dirigió a una peligrosa misión para recuperar
tierras de los indígenas norteamericanos
en la Battle of Fallen Timbers (Batalla de
Fallen Timbers) en 1794. Mil soldados de
los Estados Unidos pelearon contra 500
indígenas norteamericanos. Los soldados
ganaron y construyeron varios fuertes
nuevos a lo largo del río Ohio. El mayor
Zebulon Pike estaba al mando de uno de
esos nuevos fuertes. Durante los cuatro años
que siguieron, Zebulon fue consignado
a otros fuertes militares y trabajó en el
departamento de suministros. El conoció a
su mujer, Clarissa, en un fuerte militar. Se
casaron en 1801. Tuvieron varios hijos, pero
sólo una hija sobrevivió. Su familia vivió con

él en los fuertes pero no fueron capaces de acompañarle en sus peligrosas expediciones.

Un evento muy importante ocurrió durante esta época en la historia norteamericana. El emperador de Francia, Napoleón Bonaparte, ofreció vender las tierras entre el Mississippi River (Río Mississippi) y las Rocky Mountains (Montañas Rocosas) a los Estados Unidos. Los americanos aceptaron la oferta, y de repente, el tamaño de los Estados Unidos se duplicó. El **territorio** fue llamado la Louisiana Purchase (Compra de Luisiana). En 1804, el presidente Thomas Jefferson envió a dos exploradores llamados Lewis y Clark para que exploraran la parte norte del nuevo territorio. En 1805, el general James Wilkinson envió a Zebulon Pike a encontrar la **naciente** del Mississippi River.

Se suponía que Pike y sus hombres debían volver a St. Louis antes de que comenzara el invierno pero se quedaron más tiempo durante el frío clima. Sus soldados tenían

AN ACCOUNT OF EXPEDITIONS

TO THE

Sources of the Mississippi,

AND THROUGH THE

WESTERN PARTS OF LOUISIANA,

TO THE SOURCES OF THE

ARKANSAW, KANS, LA PLATTE, AND PIERRE JAUN, RIVERS:

PERFORMED BY ORDER OF THE

GOVERNMENT OF THE UNITED STATES

DURING THE YEARS 1805, 1806, AND 1807.

AND A TOUR THROUGH

THE

INTERIOR PARTS OF NEW SPAIN,

WHEN CONDUCTED THROUGH THESE PROVINCES,

BY ORDER OF

THE CAPTAIN-GENERAL,

IN THE YEAR 1807.

BY MAJOR Z. M. PIKE.

ILLUSTRATED BY MAPS AND CHARTS.

PHILADELPHIA:

PUBLISHED BY C. & A. CONRAD, & Co. No. 30, CHESNUT STREET. SOMERVELL & CONRAD, PETERSBURGH. BONSAL, CONRAD, & Co. NORFOLK. AND FIELDING LUCAS, Jr. BALTIMORE.

John Binns, Printer. 1810.

Zebulon Pike llevaba consigo un diario durante sus expediciones del oeste. Su diario fue publicado como el libro. Este diario fue titulado An Account of Expeditions to the Sources of the Mississippi and through the Western Parts of Louisiana... and a Tour through the Interior Parts of New Spain *(Relato de una Expedición al Nacimiento del Mississippi y a través de la Parte Occidental de Luisiana...y un Tour a través del Interior de la Nueva España).*

6 *Zebulon Pike*

3d December, Wednesday.—The weather moderating to 3 below 0, our absentees joined, one with his feet frozen, but were not able to bring up the horse; sent two men back on horseback. The hardships of last voyage had now began, and had the climate only been as severe as the climate then was, some of the men must have perished, for they had no winter clothing; I wore myself cotton overalls, for I had not calculated on being out in that inclement season of the year. Dr. Robinson and myself, with assistants, went out and took the altitude of the north mountain, on the base of a mile;* after which, together with Sparks, we endeavoured to kill a *cow* but without effect. Killed two bulls, that the men might use pieces of their hides for mockinsons. Left Sparks out. On our return to camp found the men had got back with the strayed horse, but too late to march.

4th December, Thursday.—Marched about five; took up Sparks who had succeeded in killing a cow. Killed two buffalo and six turkies. Distance 20 miles.

5th December, Friday.—Marched at our usual hour. Passed one very bad place of *falling rocks*; had to carry our loads. Encamped on the main branch of the river, near the entrance of the south mountain. In the evening walked up to the mountain. Heard 14 guns at camp during my absence, which alarmed me considerably; returned as quickly as possible, and found that the cause of my

* The perpendicular height of the mountain from the level of the prairie, was 10,581 feet, and admitting that the prairie was 8000 feet from the level of the sea, it would make the elevation of this peak 18,581 feet, equal to some, and surpassing the calculated height of others, for the peak of Teneriffe and falling short of that of Chimborazo only 1,701 feet. Indeed it was so remarkable as to be known to all the savage nation for hundreds of miles around, and to be spoken of with admiration by the Spaniards of N. Mexico, and was the bounds of their travels N. W. Indeed in our wandering in the mountains, it was never out of our sight, (except when in a valley) from the 14th November to the 27th January.

poca comida y sólo algunas piezas de equipo.
Remaron en un barco de madera de 75 pies
contra una fuerte corriente río arriba por
el Mississippi River. A veces, tuvieron que
tirar del pesado barco río arriba con cuerdas.
Zebulon no sabía lo que le esperaba en la larga
y difícil travesía. El y sus soldados llevaban
puesto abrigos ligeros de algodón, botas
delgadas y camisas largas. Tenían mucho frío
porque las temperaturas bajaban de cero con
frecuencia. La mayor parte de la carne que
comían provenía del venado que cazaban.
Los comerciantes indígenas norteamericanos
y británicos ayudaron a Zebulon y a sus
hombres a sobrevivir dándoles comida y
refugio. No encontraron la verdadera fuente
del Mississippi River. Sin embargo, Zebulon
les compró tierras a los indios sioux. Más
adelante las ciudades de Minneapolis y St.
Paul, en Minnesota, fueron construidas en
estas tierras.

Poco después de que Zebulon regresara de su exploración del Mississippi River, el general Wilkinson le ordenó explorar la zona que hoy en día son Colorado y New Mexico. Viajó desde 1805 a 1806 a lo largo de lo que hoy son los actuales estados de Missouri, Kansas, Colorado y New Mexico. Esta tierra era parte del **Louisiana Territory (Territorio de Luisiana)**. España era la propietaria de las tierras que se encontraban al oeste de este territorio. Se avisó a las tropas españolas sobre la expedición de Pike e intentaron capturarlo, pero no lo lograron.

Explorando a Colorado y a New Mexico (Nuevo México)

¡Los soldados no estaban bien preparados para un viaje tan frío! Sólo llevaban ropas de verano. Zebulon escribió en su **diario** el 3 de diciembre de 1806:

> **La temperatura más alta** llegaba a 3 grados bajo cero, y ellos [sus soldados] no tenían ropas de invierno. Yo mismo llevaba puesto sobretodos de algodón ya que no tenía pensado estar a la intemperie durante esa **inclemente** estación del año.

Llevaban mocasines de cuero fino, por lo que muchos soldados acabaron con **lesiones de congelación** en los pies. En enero de 1806, los hombres escalaron las Sangre de Cristo Mountains (Montañas Sangre de Cristo) en el San Luis Valley (Valle de San Luis). Las temperaturas llegaban a bajo cero, y en

ocasiones tenían que caminar hundidos hasta la cintura a través de la nieve. Los soldados hacían grandes fogatas por la noche para mantenerse calientes. Viajaban sólo entre cinco a diez millas por día, bastante menos que las 20 millas que solían recorrer al día. Con frecuencia tenían muy poca comida o casi ninguna. En una ocasión, no comieron durante tres días. Los hombres estaban muertos de hambre, pasando un frío extremo y estaban cansados.

Construyeron otro fuerte al sur de lo que hoy en día es Alamosa. Unos días más tarde, las tropas españolas llegaron y les preguntaron por qué estaban en territorio Español. Pike se hizo el que no sabía que estaba en tierras pertenecientes a los españoles y fue con ellos hasta Santa Fé, luego a Chihuahua, Mexico, para contestar a más preguntas.

Los españoles trataron bien a Pike y a sus hombres y les dejaron regresar a los Estados

Pikes Peak

Después de viajar a través de Missouri y Kansas, se le ordenó a Zebulon que regresara a St. Louis antes del invierno, pero continuó dirigiéndose hacia el oeste. Él y sus hombres llegaron a una zona a unas 90 millas de lo que hoy en día es Denver, cerca del lugar donde estaría la ciudad de Pueblo en el futuro. Allí, construyeron un pequeño fuerte de leños. Fue la primera construcción americana en Colorado. Desde el fuerte, divisaron una alta montaña coronada

Cortesía de DPL, Western History Collection, CHS.J2

En 1806, Zebulon Pike y sus hombres fueron los primeros norteamericanos en ver la montaña que él llamó Grand Peak. Hoy en día, a esa montaña la llamamos Pikes Peak.

Pike y sus hombres enfrentaron condiciones muy frías y malas cuando trataron de escalar Pikes Peak en 1860. El viaje fue tan malo que Pike escribió en su diario que nadie podría llegar hasta la cima. Esta fotografía de los escaladores fue tomada durante su travesía a la cima alrededor de 1950.

de nieve. Zebulon la llamó Grand Peak (Pico Grande). Pensó que podría escalar hasta la cima en un día. Pike y sus hombres hicieron una larga caminata durante tres días, pero estaban aún a diez millas de la cumbre. Pike escribió que sería imposible para cualquier persona poder escalar hasta la cima debido a la profundidad de la nieve y a las gélidas temperaturas. A esta montaña se le conoce hoy como Pikes Peak, y muchas personas escalan hasta su cumbre cada año.

Unidos. En su viaje de regreso, Zebulon escribió sobre lo que vio en los fuertes y pueblos españoles. En esta información incluyó qué tan grandes eran los fuertes, cuántos soldados había en ellos y qué tipo de murallas militares habían construido alrededor de los mismos. Sus hombres comerciaron con joyas, comida y **baratijas** con los indígenas norteamericanos durante su travesía.

Zebulon permaneció con su familia en el fuerte de St. Louis durante varios años. Trabajó muy duro en el ejército y se ganó el rango de brigadier general. Cuando comenzó la War of 1812 (La Guerra de 1812) entre los Estados Unidos y Gran Bretaña, Zebulon dirigió a sus hombres hacia el peligro una vez más. En el año 1813, durante la Battle of York (Batalla de York) cerca de Toronto, Canadá, el brigadier general Pike fue asesinado. Tenía 34 años de edad cuando murió.

El legado de Pike

Zebulon Pike jugó un papel muy importante en la historia de los Estados Unidos y de Colorado. Dirigió dos expediciones importantes: encontrar el nacimiento del Mississippi River y trazar mapas de los nuevos territorios del oeste en Nuevo México y Colorado. Describió grandes zonas del oeste norteamericano y abrió estas tierras para los futuros **asentamientos**. Tuvo poco contacto con los indígenas norteamericanos ya que el territorio que exploró estaba **habitado** por una u otra tribu que se desplazaban de un lado al otro, y no vivían en aldeas establecidas. Peleó valientemente durante la War of 1812 y murió defendiendo a los Estados Unidos.

Zebulon fue el primer norteamericano en describir Pikes Peak, montaña a la que futuros exploradores le pusieron su nombre. Muchos años después, Katharine Lee Bates escribió

un poema después de contemplar una vista **inspiradora** desde la cumbre de Pikes Peak. Más adelante se compuso música usando sus palabras como letra. La canción se llama "America the Beautiful". Estas son las primeras cuatro líneas:

¡Oh! preciosa por tus vastos cielos,
Por esos granos de ondulante ámbar,
Por tus majestuosas montañas violetas
¡Que se levantan por encima de llanuras
fructíferas!

Preguntas en qué pensar

- Tal y como hizo Pike, ¿estarías dispuesto a enlistarte en el ejército a los 15 años de edad? ¿Por qué sí o no?

- ¿Por qué Zebulon pensó que nadie podría llegar a escalar hasta la cima del Pikes Peak?

- Tal y como hizo Pike, ¿cuánto tiempo tomaría caminar desde New Jersey hasta Colorado?

Preguntas para los Jóvenes Chautauquans

- ¿Por qué se me recuerda (o debo ser recordado) a través de la historia?

- ¿A qué adversidades me enfrenté y cómo las superé?

- ¿Cuál es mi contexto histórico? (¿Qué más sucedía en la época en que yo vivía?)

Glosario

American Revolutionary War (Guerra de la Revolución Norteamericana): guerra que se llevó a cabo entre 1775 y 1783 entres las 13 colonias y Gran Bretaña; también se le llamó la Guerra de Independencia Norteamericana.

Asentamientos: nuevos lugares colonizados por personas para vivir.

Baratijas: objetos pequeños y de poco valor.

Cima: la parte más alta de una montaña.

Diario: documentación diaria de sucesos.

Escalar: subir hasta la cima de una montaña.

Expediciones: viajes realizados por un grupo de personas con el propósito de hacer un descubrimiento.

Habitado: lugar poblado por personas.

Inclemente: tormentso y frio.

Inspiradora: situación que ocasiona emociones y sentimientos fuertes y positivos.

La temperatura más alta ("moderating"): forma antigua de decir "calentar."

Lesiones de congelación: lesiones causadas por el frío extremo.

Louisiana Territory (Territorio de Luisiana): parte central de los Estados Unidos formada por la tierra que se le compró a Francia en 1803.

Naciente: lugar donde nace una masa de agua como por ejemplo un río.

Rastreo: seguir señales, a veces huellas de pisadas, para encontrar animales y personas.

Territorio: área de tierra extensa.

Glosario

Línea cronológica

1779
Pike nació en
Lamberton, New Jersey.

1775–1783
Se llevó a cabo la
Guerra de la Revolución
Norteamericana.

1793
Pike se mudó al
Fort Washington, Ohio,
con su padre.

1794
Pike se enlistó en el
United States Army a
la edad de 15 años. Los
soldados norteamericanos
derrotaron a los indígenas
norteamericanos en la Battle
of Fallen Timbers.

1801
Pike se casó con
Clarissa Brown.

1805
Pike dirigió la Mississippi
Valley Expedition
(Expedición del Valle
del Mississippi) para
encontrar el nacimiento
del Mississippi River.

Línea cronológica

1806

Pike dirigió la Southwest Expedition (Expedición del Suroeste) para explorar y trazar mapas de la región de las Rocky Mountains de Colorado. Lewis y Clark regresaron de su expedición en tierras del noroeste.

1812

Comenzó la War of 1812 contra los británicos. Pike ascendió al rango de brigadier general.

1813

Pike murió en la Battle of York.

Bibliografía

Calvert, Patricia. *Zebulon Pike—Lost in the Rockies.* New York: Benchmark Books, 2003.

Doak, Robin S. *Zebulon Pike: Explorer and Soldier.* Minneapolis: Compass Point Books, 2006.

Pike National Historic Trail Association. *Pike, The Real Pathfinder.* http://zebulonpike.org.

Pike, Zebulon. *The Expeditions of Zebulon Montgomery Pike Through Louisiana Territory and in New Spain During the Years 1805-6-7.* Minneapolis: Ross & Haines, 1965.

Pike, Zebulon. *The Southwestern Journals of Zebulon Pike.* Albuquerque: University of New Mexico Press, 2006.

Sanford, William, and Carl Green. *Zebulon Pike: Explorer of the Southwest.* Springfield, New Jersey: Enslow Publishers, 1996.

Sinnot, Susan. *The World's Great Explorers.* Chicago: Children's Press, 1990.

Stallones, Jared. *Zebulon Pike and the Explorers of the American Southwest.* New York/Philadelphia: Chelsea House Publishers, 1992.

Witteman, Barbara. *Zebulon Pike: Soldier and Explorer.* Mankato, Minnesota: Bridgestone Books, 2003.

Índice

Sobre esta serie

En 2008, Colorado Humanities y el Departamento
de Estudios Sociales de las Escuelas Públicas de
Denver (DPS) iniciaron una asociación para ofrecer el
programa Young Chautauqua de Colorado Humanities
en DPS y crear una serie de biografías de personajes
históricos de Colorado escritas por maestros para
jóvenes lectores. Al proyecto se le llamó "Writing
Biographies for Young People." Filter Press se unió al
esfuerzo para publicar las biografías en 2010.

Los maestros asistieron a seminarios, aprendieron
de conferenciantes y autores Chautauqua de Colorado
Humanities y recorrieron tres grandes bibliotecas de
Denver: La Biblioteca Hart en History Colorado,
el Departamento de Historia del Oeste/Genealogía
de la Biblioteca Pública de Denver y la Biblioteca
Blair-Caldwell de Investigaciones Afro-americanas.
La meta era escribir biografías usando las mismas
aptitudes que les pedimos a los estudiantes: identificar
y ubicar fuentes de información de alta calidad para la
investigación, documentar esas fuentes de información
y seleccionar la información apropiada contenida en
las fuentes de información.

Lo que tienes ahora en tus manos es la
culminación de los esfuerzos de estos maestros. Con
esta colección de biografías apropiadas para los jóvenes
lectores, los estudiantes podrán leer e investigar por sí
solos, aprender aptitudes valiosas para la investigación,
y escribir a temprana edad. Mientras leen cada una de
las biografías, los estudiantes obtienen conocimientos
y aprecio por los esfuerzos y adversidades superadas

por la gente de nuestro pasado, el período en el que vivieron y el porqué deben ser recordados en la historia.

El conocimiento es poder. Esperamos que este conjunto de biografías ayude a que los estudiantes de Colorado se den cuenta de la emoción que se siente al aprender historia a través de las biografías.

Se puede obtener información sobre esta serie de cualquiera de estos tres socios:

Filter Press en www.FilterPressBooks.com

Colorado Humanities en www.ColoradoHumanities.org

Escuelas Públicas de Denver en http://curriculum.dpsk12.org

Reconocimientos

Colorado Humanities y las Escuelas Públicas de
Denver hacen un reconocimiento a las muchas personas
y organizaciones que ha contribuido para hacer realidad
la serie Grandes vidas en la Historia de Colorado. Entre
ellas se encuentran:

Los maestros que aceptaron el reto de escribir las
    biografías
Margaret Coval, Directora Ejecutiva de Colorado
    Humanities
Josephine Jones, Directora de Programas de Colorado
    Humanities
Betty Jo Brenner, Coordinadora de Programas de
    Colorado Humanities
Michelle Delgado, Coordinadora de Estudios Sociales
    para kindergarten a 5º grado, de las Escuelas Públicas
    de Denver
Elma Ruiz, Coordinadora de Estudios Sociales 2005-
    2009, para kindergarten a 5º grado, de las Escuelas
    Públicas de Denver
Joel' Bradley, Coordinador de Proyectos de las Escuelas
    Públicas de Denver
El equipo de Servicios de Traducción e Interpretación, de
    la Oficina de Enlaces Multiculturales de las Escuelas
    Públicas de Denver
Nelson Molina, Preparador/entrenador del programa de
    Capacitación Profesional de ELA y Persona de Enlace
    Escolar de las Escuelas Públicas de Denver
John Stansfield, narrador de cuentos, escritor y líder
    experto del Instituto para maestros

Tom Meier, autor e historiador de los Arapaho

Celinda Reynolds Kaelin, autora y experta en la cultura Ute

National Park Service, Sitio Histórico Nacional Bent's Old Fort

Daniel Blegen, autor y experto en Bent's Fort

Biblioteca de Investigaciones Afroamericanas Blair-Caldwell

Coi Drummond-Gehrig, Departamento de Historia/ Genealogía Occidental de la Biblioteca Pública de Denver

Jennifer Vega, Biblioteca Stephen H., de History Colorado

Dr. Bruce Paton, autor y experto Zebulon Pike

Dr. Tom Noel, autor e historiador de Colorado

Susan Marie Frontczak, oradora chautauqua y capacitadora de la Juventud Chautauqua

Mary Jane Bradbury, oradora chautauqua y capacitadora de la Juventud Chautauqua

Dr. James Walsh, orador chautauqua y capacitador de la Juventud Chautauqua

Richard Marold, orador chautauqua y capacitador de la Juventud Chautauqua

Doris McCraw, autora y experta en materia de Helen Hunt Jackson

Kathy Naples, oradora chautauqua y experta en materia de Doc Susie

Tim Brenner, editor

Debra Faulkner, historiadora y archivista, Hotel Brown Palace

Kathleen Esmiol, autora y oradora del Instituto de Maestros Vivian Sheldon Epstein, autora y oradora del Instituto de Maestros

Beth Kooima, diseñador gráfico, Kooima Kreations